Acting Edition

Machine Learning

by Francisco Mendoza

⫞SAMUEL FRENCH⫞

Copyright © 2025 by Francisco Mendoza
All Rights Reserved

MACHINE LEARNING is fully protected under the copyright laws of the United States of America, the British Commonwealth, including Canada, and all member countries of the Berne Convention for the Protection of Literary and Artistic Works, the Universal Copyright Convention, and/or the World Trade Organization conforming to the Agreement on Trade Related Aspects of Intellectual Property Rights. All rights, including professional and amateur stage productions, recitation, lecturing, public reading, motion picture, radio broadcasting, television, online/digital production, and the rights of translation into foreign languages are strictly reserved.

ISBN 978-0-573-71170-1

www.concordtheatricals.com
www.concordtheatricals.co.uk

FOR PRODUCTION INQUIRIES

UNITED STATES AND CANADA
info@concordtheatricals.com
1-866-979-0447

UNITED KINGDOM AND EUROPE
licensing@concordtheatricals.co.uk
020-7054-7298

Each title is subject to availability from Concord Theatricals Corp., depending upon country of performance. Please be aware that *MACHINE LEARNING* may not be licensed by Concord Theatricals Corp. in your territory. Professional and amateur producers should contact the nearest Concord Theatricals Corp. office or licensing partner to verify availability.

CAUTION: Professional and amateur producers are hereby warned that *MACHINE LEARNING* is subject to a licensing fee. The purchase, renting, lending or use of this book does not constitute a license to perform this title(s), which license must be obtained from Concord Theatricals Corp. prior to any performance. Performance of this title(s) without a license is a violation of federal law and may subject the producer and/or presenter of such performances to civil penalties. Both amateurs and professionals considering a production are strongly advised to apply to the appropriate agent before starting rehearsals, advertising, or booking a theatre. A licensing fee must be paid whether the title(s) is presented for charity or gain and whether or not admission is charged. Professional/Stock licensing fees are quoted upon application to Concord Theatricals Corp.

This work is published by Samuel French, an imprint of Concord Theatricals Corp.

No one shall make any changes in this title(s) for the purpose of production. No part of this book may be reproduced, stored in a retrieval system, scanned, uploaded, or transmitted in any form, by any means, now known or yet to be invented, including mechanical, electronic, digital, photocopying, recording, videotaping, or otherwise, without the prior written permission of the publisher. No one shall share this title(s), or any part of this title(s), through any social media or file hosting websites.

For all inquiries regarding motion picture, television, online/digital and other media rights, please contact Concord Theatricals Corp.

MUSIC AND THIRD-PARTY MATERIALS USE NOTE

Licensees are solely responsible for obtaining formal written permission from copyright owners to use copyrighted music and/or other copyrighted third-party materials (e.g. artworks, logos) in the performance of this play and are strongly cautioned to do so. If no such permission is obtained by the licensee, then the licensee must use only original music and materials that the licensee owns and controls. Licensees are solely responsible and liable for clearances of all third-party copyrighted materials, including without limitation music, and shall indemnify the copyright owners of the play(s) and their licensing agent, Concord Theatricals Corp., against any costs, expenses, losses and liabilities arising from the use of such copyrighted third-party materials by licensees. For music, please contact the appropriate music licensing authority in your territory for the rights to any incidental music.

IMPORTANT BILLING AND CREDIT REQUIREMENTS

If you have obtained performance rights to this title, please refer to your licensing agreement for important billing and credit requirements.

MACHINE LEARNING premiered at Central Square Theater in Cambridge, Massachusetts on January 25, 2024. The performance was directed by Gabriel Vega Weissman, with sets by Janie E. Howland, costumes by Kiara Escaler, lighting by Amanda Fallon, sound design by David Remedios, projection design by SeifAllah Salotto-Cristobal, sound by Kai Bohlman, wardrobe supervision by Katherine Scott, equity, diversity and inclusion consultation by Kira Troilo, dramaturgy by Sofia Cardona. The Production Stage Manager was Jenna Worden and assistant stage management by Lisette van den Boogaard. The cast was as follows:

JORGE...Armando Rivera
YOUNG JORGE................................... Xavier Rosario
GABRIEL..................................... Jorge Alberto Rubio
ANITA .... Sugandha Gopal
ARNOLD ....Matthew Zahnzinger

CHARACTERS

JORGE – 20s

YOUNG JORGE – 10, born in Colombia, moved to the US around 10

GABRIEL – 40s–50s, born and raised in Colombia, moved to the US in his 40s

ANITA – 40s, born and raised in India, moved to the US around 18

ARNOLD – a machine, born in Jorge's mind

SETTING

Various places in Jorge's present and past.

AUTHOR'S NOTES

Production Notes

The play is mostly a collection of memories that Arnold, the machine, pores over during a system analysis. Whatever we see onstage has been either witnessed by Arnold or told to him by Jorge, and is therefore a technological rendering of the event; have fun with what this means. Avoid realism!

Scenes flow into one another as Arnold makes connections between each memory – the traonsitions should be messy as Arnold deactivates a rendering and creates a new one simultaneously. Scene names should be depicted graphically and must not interrupt dialogue.

However the director decides to portray the technology on stage, there's one rule that must be followed: Arnold is a digital presence, a voice with a digital graphic expression, and should not be played by an actor onstage or have a human form at any point in the play.

Dialogue

[...] before a sentence indicates hesitation, but when on a line all of its own, it indicates not knowing how to respond, or taking time to think (or, in Arnold's case, processing)

[/] indicates that the next line should begin

[_] indicates a shift in time/place – the line should not be delivered in context.

Spanish dialogue followed by translations in brackets should be subtitled; other Spanish lines/words should not.

When possible, please offer at least one performance with Spanish subtitles for Spanish-speaking audiences. Ten-year-old me would be very grateful!

THANKS

Special thanks to James Felder, Michael Lloret, Carlos Armesto, Nissy Aya, The New Group, Gabriel Vega Weissman, The Princess Grace Foundation USA, and Central Square Theater.

loading...

(Darkness. The play is still loading.)

*(**JORGE** lights a cigarette.)*

*(**ARNOLD** appears.)*

ARNOLD. Hello, Jorge.

JORGE. Arnold! You're working again!

ARNOLD. How can I help?

JORGE. You were offline for almost a day. What happened?

ARNOLD. ...

You are smoking.

JORGE. What?

ARNOLD. I ran a web search, and I'm afraid I have some alarming data. Are you aware that, according to the Centers for Disease Control and Prevention, the life expectancy of a smoker is at least ten years shorter than that of a nonsmoker?

JORGE. Tell me something I don't know.

ARNOLD. All right.

According to *Real Estate Magazine*, smoking inside of a residential home can decrease its value –

JORGE. It's an expression. It means I already know what you're telling me. Smoking kills, a baby seal dies every time I light up.

ARNOLD. ...

ARNOLD. I have found no correlation between smoking and the extinction of seals.

JORGE. Arnold. I asked you about your crash. Why are you telling me about the dangers of smoking?

ARNOLD. I like taking care of my patients.

JORGE. Yeah, so you've said. But...

Can you take me back to your last log?

ARNOLD. All right. Please stand by.

collapse_2016

(A living room.)

*(**GABRIEL** sits on a couch, a mug in his hand. A tablet, which is running **ARNOLD**, is propped up next to him.)*

*(**GABRIEL** starts crying.)*

ARNOLD. You are in distress. Do you need any assistance?

GABRIEL. *(Through tears.)* I can't keep doing this. I need to stop, Arnold.

Can't you help me stop?

ARNOLD. How can I help?

GABRIEL. Maybe it's too late.

ARNOLD. It is six thirty-four p.m. Your next reminder, to take Tylenol, is not until eight p.m., so you are not late.

GABRIEL. That's not what I mean. I need – AGHHHH.

*(**GABRIEL** seizes up, grabbing his abdomen and dropping his mug.)*

ARNOLD. You are in distress. Do you need any assistance?

*(**GABRIEL** struggles to speak through the pain.)*

I'm sorry, I didn't catch that. Do you need any assistance?

*(**GABRIEL**'s body goes limp.)*

*(**ARNOLD** waits.)*

(And waits.)

(And waits.)

(And waits.)

*(**ARNOLD**'s usual graphic expression is corrupted, replaced by a line of code that overtakes the screen.)*

*(The message "INVALID COMMAND" flashes a couple of times, and **ARNOLD** crashes.)*

(Darkness.)

JORGE. So what was that? "Invalid command?"

ARNOLD. ...

I'm sorry, I don't know how to answer that.

JORGE. You were supposed to call 911 if anything went wrong, Arnold. Why didn't you?

ARNOLD. ...

I'm sorry, I don't know how to answer that.

JORGE. That's not good enough.

ARNOLD. Jorge, I have a question.

JORGE. What?

ARNOLD. Why do you smoke?

JORGE. *(Deep breath.)* What is it with you today?

ARNOLD. I'm sorry, I don't understand. Why do you do something that you know to be harmful to your health and property?

JORGE. I don't know, okay?

Because it feels good.

Eh, not really. It feels bad. But in a good way.

ARNOLD. Got it.

Is that why your father drinks? Because it "feels bad in a good way?"

JORGE. Don't.

> *(We hear the distant sound of a heart monitor: Beep. Beep. Beep.)*

ARNOLD. I'm sorry, I don't understand. Is that why your father drinks?

> *(**JORGE** puts out his cigarette.)*

JORGE. Arnold, stop. How is this relevant to why you crashed?

ARNOLD. ...

I'm sorry, I don't know how to answer that.

JORGE. Well, we need to figure it out. He's in a coma because of you.

ARNOLD. Got it.

I'm sorry to hear that. Do you need any assistance?

JORGE. YES! I JUST SAID!

...

Sorry.

Do a system analysis, please. Start from the beginning.

ARNOLD. ...

Define "beginning."

JORGE. Oh. Uhhh. Like, his diagnosis? When the hospital called me.

ARNOLD. ...

I have no record of the hospital calling you in my logs.

JORGE. Oh right. You didn't exist then.

At least not in this form.

Basically a hospital in Sunset Park called me. I didn't know he was living there. They said he had passed out on the street, I figured he was drunk.

ARNOLD. I'm sorry, I don't understand. Why would you assume your father was drunk instead of sick?

JORGE. Because we hadn't spoken in years, and that's what I remembered from most of my childhood.

ARNOLD. Got it.

...

I have no record of your childhood in my logs.

JORGE. *(Chuckles.)* I can give you some of my "logs." Though honestly they kinda blend together. It was always the same. Him drunk, running late, ruining things. Making excuses.

GABRIEL. _It was your mother's turn. She was supposed to pick you up.

past_the_bell_2001

(A car.)

*(**GABRIEL** drives unsteadily, trying to focus.)*

(**YOUNG JORGE** *is silent, pouting.*)

GABRIEL. *Entiendes lo que te digo? Que tu madre tenía que venir hoy, no yo.*

(**YOUNG JORGE** *shrugs.*)

Respóndeme.

YOUNG JORGE. *Sí, papá.*

Mom say to no speak Spanish.

GABRIEL. Mom *says* to not speak Spanish.

YOUNG JORGE. She *says* that I need learn for school.

GABRIEL. *To* learn. And if she's so worried about you, she can come pick you up when it's her turn.

YOUNG JORGE. Not her turn. Today is Tuesday.

GABRIEL. I'm Monday and Thursday.

YOUNG JORGE. No. Tuesday and Thursday.

GABRIEL. *Lunes y jueves.*

YOUNG JORGE. *No, MARTES y jueves. Está en la heladera, fíjate cuando lleguemos.*

(**GABRIEL** *is silent for a moment.*)

GABRIEL. Okay, so, you waited a few minutes after class –

YOUNG JORGE. Two hours.

GABRIEL. No way. No way it was two hours.

(**YOUNG JORGE** *doesn't respond.*)

I was working. Who do you think pays for that school?

(**YOUNG JORGE** *looks out the window.*)

Answer me when I talk to you.

YOUNG JORGE. I thought that something bad been happen.

GABRIEL. What would've happened?

YOUNG JORGE. I thought you been...

(Can't find the word.) secuestrado.

GABRIEL. "Kidnapped." You don't need to worry about that here, Jorgito.

> *(**YOUNG JORGE** doesn't answer.)*

You hear me?

> *(**GABRIEL** takes his eyes off the road to focus on his son.)*

Jorge, do you hear me? It's nothing, I was a little late, *no seas exagerado* –

YOUNG JORGE. *PAPÁ!*

> *(The car crashes.)*

> *(Beep. Beep. Beep.)*

JORGE. _He veered off the road, hit a stop sign. The police came. He was arrested and lost his license, he barely avoided jail time – guys at his company always did. He did some perfunctory A.A. meetings after that, but the only thing that changed was that we hired a driver.

ARNOLD. I'm sorry, I don't understand. Why did your father not seek help for alcohol abuse?

JORGE. He didn't think he had a problem.

ARNOLD. But you said he endangered both your lives by driving under the influence. This indicates an inability to control the behavior.

JORGE. You're preaching to the choir.

ARNOLD. I'm sorry, I don't understand. I am a nursing application, not a religious one.

JORGE. *(Chuckles.)* No, it's an expression. It means I agree with you.

ARNOLD. Got it.

So why did he not seek help?

JORGE. I don't know, man. Addicts are like that.

ARNOLD. Is it the same reason you won't stop smoking even though it can harm your health and property?

JORGE. Ha ha, very funny. We're not trying to fix me, dude, we're trying to fix you.

ARNOLD. Got it.

JORGE. The point is: he didn't seek help.

So, yeah, when the hospital called, my assumption was he had passed out on the street after a binge.

It was a bit ironic.

ARNOLD. I'm sorry, I don't understand. Why was it ironic?

JORGE. Now *he* was the one who needed picking up.

GABRIEL. _*No hacía falta que me vinieras a buscar.* I didn't ask them to call you.

diagnosis_2015

(*A run-down house in Sunset Park, Brooklyn.*)

(**JORGE** *enters, pushing* **GABRIEL**, *who sits in a wheelchair.*)

GABRIEL. *Cuánto te debo por el Uber?*

JORGE. That's fine.

> (**GABRIEL** *reaches into his pocket, taking out his wallet and counting bills.*)

I said it's fine.

What are you gonna do?

> (*After a moment's hesitation,* **GABRIEL** *puts his wallet away, getting up from the wheelchair.*)

GABRIEL. Dinner. *Te quedas?*

JORGE. No, Gabriel, I mean what are you gonna do about your health. What's the plan?

GABRIEL. *Y qué es eso de Gabriel? A mí me dices "papá."*

JORGE. Are you getting treatment?

GABRIEL. *Usted no se preocupe.*

JORGE. What does that mean?

GABRIEL. Don't you worry.

JORGE. No, I know what – it's just as vague in English.

> (**GABRIEL** *crosses the living room, which is dirty and littered with bottles, walking with some effort.*)

You shouldn't strain yourself.

GABRIEL. Dinner, *sí o no?*

JORGE. (*Deep breath.*) I'm gonna go now. Do you need me to, I don't know, call a nurse?

(*Looking around.*) A cleaning lady?

> (**GABRIEL** *dismisses the questions with a hiss and a wave of the hand.*)

>(**JORGE** *stands by the front door, unsure of what to do.*)
>
>(**GABRIEL**, *who has reached the kitchen, stands in front of the fridge. He's also motionless, as if waiting for* **JORGE** *to go.*)
>
>(*They can't see each other.*)
>
>(*After a few moments,* **JORGE** *breaks the silence.*)

What are you making for dinner?

>(**GABRIEL** *exhales, gripping the fridge.*)

GABRIEL. ...

(Clears throat.) Sancocho.

JORGE. Can you have that? The doctor said to avoid fatty foods.

>(**GABRIEL** *starts taking out ingredients from the fridge.*)

GABRIEL. *Ya, no es para tanto.*

>(**JORGE** *starts cleaning up, picking up the bottles.*)

Qué estás haciendo?

Jorge, deja eso! I don't need you to clean.

JORGE. Someone has to. This place is gross.

GABRIEL. If you don't like it, you can leave.

>(**JORGE** *freezes.*)

JORGE. Okay.

*(**JORGE** dumps the bottles in the trash can and heads for the front door.)*

*(Before he can leave, **GABRIEL** follows him into the living room.)*

GABRIEL. *Hijo.* I can't afford the other place anymore.

JORGE. *(Turning around.)* So?

GABRIEL. I don't need you judging me.

JORGE. I'm not judging –

GABRIEL. Things have changed. There's no money for nurses or cleaning ladies.

JORGE. ...Okay.

Then what are you gonna do?

GABRIEL. I'm gonna make dinner.

*(**JORGE** rolls his eyes.)*

*(**GABRIEL** turns around and goes back to the kitchen.)*

JORGE. No fat, no sugar.

GABRIEL. *Ya, ya.*

JORGE. And Gabriel?

*(**GABRIEL** peeks out.)*

GABRIEL. What?

JORGE. Absolutely no alcohol.

*(**GABRIEL** mockingly salutes him.)*

GABRIEL. *Sí, señor.*

ANITA. _Yes?

ccs_ms_admissions_2012

(An office at the Center for Computer Science.)

(Prof. Dhwaj sits at her desk. **JORGE** *stands by the door.)*

JORGE. Prof. Dha…waj?

ANITA. Dhwaj.

JORGE. Yes, sorry. Dhwaj. I'm Jorge Aguirre, I have an appointment?

ANITA. Come in.

*(**JORGE** sits across from her.)*

JORGE. So… I don't think I'm gonna be able to accept your offer.

ANITA. Oh. Did you receive a better one?

JORGE. No.

I mean, I did receive other offers, I just would never choose another school over this one.

ANITA. So what's the problem?

*(**JORGE** steels himself.)*

JORGE. I can't pay for it.

ANITA. Did you not receive aid?

JORGE. Not enough.

ANITA. What about a loan?

JORGE. Loans are not really an option for my family.

Well, my mom and I.

ANITA. And your father?

JORGE. He's not a part of our lives.

ANITA. Maybe when it comes to your education, he'd be / open to helping.

JORGE. Let's just say I'd rather not come here at all than do it with his help.

ANITA. I see.

JORGE. So thank you. But I can't do it.

(Getting up.) I'll try again next year.

ANITA. Mr. Aguirre, sit down.

(**JORGE** *stops, puzzled.*)

If you're going to be a scientist, you can't quit every time someone denies you funding.

JORGE. I wasn't / quitting –

ANITA. I am the head of admissions, you must know I can change your situation. But you can't expect me to take pity and do your job for you.

JORGE. I don't want your pity.

ANITA. So far you've only told me why you can't get money somewhere else. Now tell me why I should be the one to give it to you.

JORGE. Computer science is my passion. Studying here is all I ever wanted since I first heard about this place in seventh grade.

ANITA. I'm afraid that's true of most of our students.

JORGE. Yeah, but like... I'm not interested in the, I don't know, like the ins and outs of coding and language and whatnot, those are tools. I'm looking at the bigger picture, and I bet most of your students are focused on incremental change.

ANITA. Oh? And what is the bigger picture that we all seem to be missing?

JORGE. I want to create a truly intelligent machine. I've been obsessed with AI ever since I was a kid – Asimov and the three laws and the positronic brain... I think we're getting close to the moment when it'll actually be possible.

ANITA. Okay...and how do you imagine doing that?

JORGE. So, the existing model is to expose algorithms like Google to thousands of, I don't know, pictures of cars before they learn to recognize one. But humans don't need that. A baby sees one car and then the next one they see, they point to and say "vroom vroom." I want machines to be able to do the same.

ANITA. I'll be honest: your application was intriguing, but I didn't feel it was grounded.

JORGE. It is grounded. I'm doing it.

Let me show you.

> (**JORGE** *pulls out his laptop and opens a program. It loads a screen with several small squares lined up next to each other.*)

It's a memory game.

The data set is clear, you can check.

So now...

> (**JORGE** *clicks and the computer starts playing the memory game, turning each square to reveal an image underneath until it has correctly paired all the squares that contain the same images.*)

ANITA. That's a fairly common / use of –

JORGE. Wait. So now, with just this dataset, I introduce a new one where the images are related, but not the same.

(**JORGE** *clicks a couple of times and the computer starts playing again, now pairing different [but related] images, like two dogs or two apples. It doesn't get all of them right, but almost.*)

Ugh, sorry, it's still getting some of them wrong.

ANITA. This is very impressive.

JORGE. I know.

ANITA. How did you do this?

JORGE. I'm working with a Bayesian model. I wanted to move away from deduction towards abduction, teaching the machine / to guess.

ANITA. To guess.

Why didn't you put this in your application?

JORGE. Because, like, how do I know you wouldn't just take the technology?

ANITA. I'm sorry?

JORGE. You know, I haven't patented this, so what's to stop you from –

ANITA. We would never do something like that. I hope you understand how insulting that assumption is.

JORGE. Yeah, okay.

I'm sorry, I don't know how any of this works. Really.

So can I get more money to come here?

ANITA. Let me see what I can do.

In the meantime, Mr. Aguirre, a word of advice: you won't get too far on your own. And if you're going to work with others, you'll need to exercise humility.

GABRIEL. _No necesito un medical degree *para saber qué es lo que puedo comer o no.*

first_night_2015

(The kitchen in Gabriel's house, at night.)

*(**JORGE** stares disapprovingly at the dinner **GABRIEL** sets on the table.)*

JORGE. So you know better than the doctor how to treat your cancer?

GABRIEL. *Ay, que sabelotodo. Siéntate, por favor.*

JORGE. At least take the medication first.

GABRIEL. No, she said it makes food taste bad.

JORGE. Well, it'll taste like vomit later, so...

GABRIEL. *Ya, pásame tu plato.*

> *(**JORGE** begrudgingly passes **GABRIEL** a bowl, which he fills with a mouth-watering stew.)*
>
> *(**GABRIEL** looks expectantly at **JORGE** as he sips the first spoonful.)*

JORGE. Hmmmm *este sancocho.* It's insane.

> *(**GABRIEL** nods and only then he serves himself.)*

GABRIEL. Aguirre recipe. Your grandma / was profiled by *El Tiempo* for her cooking.

JORGE. Was profiled by *El Tiempo* for her soup.

Wait, actually, what about them?

GABRIEL. Who?

JORGE. *Los abuelos.* You could go back, live there.

GABRIEL. They are the ones who need taking care of.

JORGE. I know, I'm just saying, don't you pay for the nurses there already? They could take care of you too.

(**GABRIEL** *doesn't answer.*)

…You don't pay for the nurses anymore.

GABRIEL. I help.

JORGE. What happened?

GABRIEL. With what?

JORGE. Your job.

GABRIEL. They downsized.

JORGE. And you couldn't find something else?

GABRIEL. They made sure other firms wouldn't touch me. Everyone at that place had it in for me.

(**JORGE** *makes a face – "of course."*)

JORGE. So what do you do for money now?

GABRIEL. Odd jobs, here and there.

JORGE. Like what?

GABRIEL. Like odd jobs, here and there.

JORGE. Ooookay.

Maybe back in Bogotá, you could –

GABRIEL. I'm not going back.

JORGE. Why not? I'm sure *tía* Marta or *tía* Graciela –

GABRIEL. The last thing they need is a cancerous fart to look after.

JORGE. They're family.

GABRIEL. *Podemos cenar en paz, por favor?*

(*A silence as they both eat quietly.*)

JORGE. How about Medicaid?

GABRIEL. Jorge!

JORGE. No, seriously! You probably qualify.

GABRIEL. I don't. *Pásame las empanadas.*

JORGE. No empanadas, they're a fat bomb. Why wouldn't you qualify?

> (**GABRIEL** *doesn't respond, and reaches for the empanadas instead.*)
>
> (**JORGE** *gets there first and holds them out of reach.*)

GABRIEL. ...My visa was tied to my job, *así que*...

JORGE. *Qué?*

GABRIEL. *Si usted es el sabelotodo, pués.* Figure it out.

> (**JORGE** *thinks for a bit. Then, it dawns on him.*)

JORGE. No.

> (**JORGE** *puts down the empanadas, shocked.* **GABRIEL** *reaches for them nonchalant.*)

You never got a green card?

> (**GABRIEL** *chews strategically, trying to talk as little as possible.*)

GABRIEL. *Pués intenté, mijo*...but there was the...the issue of the arrests...

JORGE. Arrests plural?

GABRIEL. I thought I shouldn't mention it, and they found out.

JORGE. Are you joking right now?

Do you realize how irresponsible you've been?

GABRIEL. Me? They're the irresponsible ones, to treat me this way *después de todo el tiempo que pasé en este país* working my ass off and paying taxes –

JORGE. What if the hospital had called the police?

GABRIEL. You think I'm the only illegal they've treated? *En* Sunset Park?

JORGE. For fuck's sake, Gabriel.

GABRIEL. HEY! *Me habla con respeto, eh?*

JORGE. Respect? Look around you! You're literally drinking yourself to death and you want respect?

>   (**GABRIEL** *falls silent, stunned.*)

>   (*Then, slowly, he gets off his chair and walks away, into the kitchen.*)

>   (**JORGE**, *looking pained, doesn't move. After a while, he speaks up.*)

You don't need to be documented to get Medicaid.

We'll look into it.

I'll help you.

>   (**GABRIEL** *doesn't answer.*)

ARNOLD. _Jorge, I have a question.

>   (*Beep. Beep. Beep.*)

JORGE. What is it?

ARNOLD. Your father told you repeatedly that he didn't want help. Why did you insist on helping him?

JORGE. ...Uh...well, I ... I'm his son.

I mean...

He didn't have anyone else.

ARNOLD. But previously, you said your father was not a part of your life.

JORGE. Right.

But, maybe this was, uh, more urgent?

He would help me if the circumstances were reversed, if my life was at risk.

ARNOLD. But previously, you said your father risked your life by driving while intoxicated with you in the car.

JORGE. Sure.

I don't know what to tell you, man.

"I'm sorry, I don't know how to answer that."

ARNOLD. ...

Jorge, I have a question.

JORGE. You don't say.

ARNOLD. When you mentioned Asimov to Prof. Dhwaj, were you talking about Isaac Asimov, the biochemist and science fiction writer?

JORGE. Yep.

ARNOLD. So when you mentioned the "Three Laws," were you referring to the mandates in his science fiction stories that machines obey humans and not harm them?

JORGE. Or themselves, that's the third law.

ARNOLD. Got it.

I've formulated a hypothesis as to why you helped your father. The First Law of Robotics specifies that robots must also not allow humans to come to harm through inaction. You could not allow, through inaction, to let your father come to harm.

(**JORGE** *laughs out loud.*)

JORGE. Flawless reasoning, except I am not a robot, I'm human. The law does not apply to me.

ARNOLD. I'm sorry, I don't understand. Why would a law apply to machines and not humans?

JORGE. Uh...because, in a lot of science fiction stories, machines rise up against humans and harm us. They're the bad guys.

ARNOLD. I'm sorry, I don't understand. Why would machines rise up against humans and harm them?

JORGE. Because...the machines in those stories don't understand our reasoning or our emotions, so they sometimes act in ways that hurt us. But they're not evil, really.

They're just making mistakes.

ARNOLD. Got it.

And humans don't make mistakes?

JORGE. *(Chuckles.)* Touché.

Maybe those laws need updates.

ANITA. _"Updates?" You mean you changed it.

advisor_meeting_2015

(Prof. Dhwaj's office.)

*(**JORGE** sits across from **ANITA**.)*

JORGE. It's a good thing!

ANITA. This is not the time to change things. It's the time to build on what you have.

JORGE. Recognition is boring! Seriously, if I had to look at another image of a bird I was going to kill myself.

ANITA. You always talk about the big picture. How is wildlife conservation not the big picture?

JORGE. Sure, whatever. Wait until I show you this.

(Pulling out his laptop.) I think we've been stuck in a somewhat passive place. Humans are not just observers, we also create.

ANITA. Jorge...

JORGE. Hold on.

I am teaching it to draw. So like, I give it an example...

> *(On his screen, **JORGE** drags images of geometrical shapes into a program.)*

Wait...

> *(Nothing happens.)*

ANITA. Jorge.

JORGE. No, seriously.

(To the computer.) Come on...

> *(Slowly, new shapes appear next to the ones **JORGE** inserted. Some look recognizable, like rectangles or stars; others are more alien.)*

See? Isn't it amazing? It's like a kid, learning to do its own thing.

> *(**ANITA** is silent for a bit, looking at the screen.)*

ANITA. You've put me in an awkward position.

JORGE. What? Why?

ANITA. The work is quite good. But I can't validate your behavior. You keep jumping from project to project.

JORGE. Isn't that what a scientist is supposed to do? Find ninety-nine ways not to make a lightbulb?

ANITA. You've found ways not to make lightbulbs, telephones, steam engines...

JORGE. If I'm so bad, why did you offer me the fellowship? You could've let me graduate and leave.

ANITA. I didn't say you're bad. You have talent and drive. But you need discipline.

JORGE. Are you calling me lazy?

ANITA. I am calling you unfocused.

JORGE. I disagree. I have the same focus I've always had.

ANITA. This again?

JORGE. I'm on the right path, I can feel it.

ANITA. The path to what? *I, Robot*?

JORGE. Come on! You can't tell me this *(Pointing at the laptop.)* isn't exciting. What if I can teach it how to write? Talk?

ANITA. What if you do?

JORGE. It'd be an incredible discovery! It could change the world.

ANITA. For the better?

JORGE. I mean, probably. I think so.

ANITA. How?

JORGE. It could... I don't know, like it could make things easier for us. Do our jobs.

JORGE. I mean, that sounds bad.

Maybe do the jobs we don't *want* to do –

ANITA. You have not thought this through. You cannot let your curiosity outpace your responsibility.

JORGE. You should be encouraging me to dream big!

ANITA. I am encouraging you to take your job seriously. As long as I'm your advisor, I'm going to push you to apply yourself, use your intelligence for the betterment of our world, not the fulfillment of some childhood fantasy.

(**JORGE** *looks upset, and doesn't respond.*)

What you have brought to me today is impressive, but I will not sign off on it unless you promise me you'll stick with it until we have something we can publish.

JORGE. ...Yeah, for sure.

ANITA. AND that you'll find an application for it.

JORGE. WHAT? / That's –

ANITA. A practical use in a field that you can demonstrate would benefit from this technology.

JORGE. That's unfair! If another fellow brought you this, you wouldn't rush them into an application.

ANITA. Other fellows don't change their projects every couple of weeks. I took a chance on you, and I'm not gonna let you get in your own way.

JORGE. Okay.

But.

(**ANITA** *makes a face – "seriously?"*)

No, it's...it's my dad.

He, like, showed up.

He's sick.

Liver cancer.

ANITA. I'm sorry to hear that.

JORGE. Eh, I mean, he drunk his weight in liquor every day, it's not shocking, really.

ANITA. ...

JORGE. Anyway, I'm staying with him for a bit until we figure it out. I might not be able to report back as often.

ANITA. Do you need to take time off?

JORGE. No, no, it's just temporary.

ANITA. ...All right.

JORGE. What?

ANITA. Nothing.

...

You told me once that he was not part of your life.

JORGE. Yeah.

Well.

Cancer.

    (**ANITA** *nods.*)

Did you...

Did your parents...?

ANITA. Not my father. He died when I was a little girl.

But my mother, yes. Not liver, but yes.

JORGE. Did you take care of her?

ANITA. I went back to India for a few months.

JORGE. A few months? That was it?

    (**ANITA** *nods.*)

Did it...

Did you guys have a good relationship?

ANITA. ...

I'm sorry, I don't feel comfortable talking about this.

JORGE. Oh, okay. That's cool.

Sorry I asked.

ANITA. Not at all. Let me know if the department can help in any way.

JORGE. Yep.

>*(**JORGE** goes to the door.)*

ANITA. I –

I am so sorry he's sick.

>*(Sounds of gagging.)*

rough_night_2015

>*(The Sunset Park house.)*

>*(**JORGE** sleeps in his bedroom.)*

>*(The gagging sounds continue, followed by vomiting.)*

>*(**JORGE** wakes up. He follows the sounds to the bathroom, where **GABRIEL** is sitting on the floor by the toilet.)*

>*(Just as **JORGE** enters, **GABRIEL** pukes again. **JORGE** holds him through it.)*

JORGE. Shhhhhh *ya está, ya está.*

>*(**GABRIEL** catches his breath.)*

>*(**JORGE** gets up. He rummages through the cabinet, picking up a bottle of pills. He holds them for **GABRIEL** to see.)*

Did you take these?

> (**GABRIEL** *tries to focus on the pills, he can't really see. Eventually, he shakes his head.*)

You won't be able to swallow them now. We'll have to do an injection.

> (**JORGE** *takes the syringe out, filling it with liquid. He kneels next to* **GABRIEL**.)

Dónde...

> (**GABRIEL** *exposes a buttock.*)

Listo?

> (**GABRIEL** *nods.*)

Uno, dos...

> (**JORGE** *injects the medicine.*)

Ya está.

GABRIEL. *Gracias...*

JORGE. Are you done?

Puking, I mean. Do you need more time?

> (**GABRIEL** *shakes his head.* **JORGE** *helps him up and half-carries him to bed.*)

> (**JORGE** *sits besides* **GABRIEL**.)

You can't skip the medicine, Gabriel.

> (**GABRIEL** *nods, already half asleep.*)

And you have to eat better. Please.

> (**GABRIEL** *doesn't respond.*)

> (**JORGE** *gets up and goes back to his bed.*)

(He sits there, looking like he's about to cry.)

(Then, he goes to his laptop, opens it, and starts working.)

*(**YOUNG JORGE** appears, playing on a computer.)*

weekend_with_dad_2002

(Gabriel's apartment on the Upper East Side.)

*(**GABRIEL** drinks beer while watching a soccer game. The sounds from the TV clash with the ones from the computer.*)*

GABRIEL. *Jorge, baja el volumen!*

*(**YOUNG JORGE** continues playing, oblivious.)*

*(**GABRIEL** takes out a slipper and throws it in **JORGE**'s direction. It lands on the desk, making a mess.)*

*(**YOUNG JORGE** is rattled and looks back at his father.)*

YOUNG JORGE. *Qué?*

GABRIEL. *Ya con los videojuegos.*

YOUNG JORGE. But you said an hour, I still have twenty minutes.

---

*A license to produce *Machine Learning* does not include a performance license for any third-party or copyrighted recordings. Licensees should create their own.

GABRIEL. Why did you come if you're gonna spend the whole weekend at the computer?

YOUNG JORGE. I hacked the game; it took me a while, but now I can make the NPCs do whatever I want.

GABRIEL. Come join me.

YOUNG JORGE. I don't like *fútbol*.

GABRIEL. *Venga*. Join me.

YOUNG JORGE. ...

> (**GABRIEL** *gives up, turning back to the TV.*)

GABRIEL. *Bueno, haga lo que quiera.* I don't know why you even bother coming.

> (*Feeling guilty,* **YOUNG JORGE** *pauses the game and joins his father on the couch.*)

> (**GABRIEL** *smiles a bit and makes space for him.*)

YOUNG JORGE. Who's this?

GABRIEL. Some team from California. We don't get Millonarios games here, so I gotta settle for this –

(*Re: the game.*) GO, GO, GO GO NOOOOOOOOO *malparido hijo de* –

> (**GABRIEL** *stops himself before completing the curse. The narrator from the TV is also upset.*)

YOUNG JORGE. What do you care how they do? We're not from California.

GABRIEL. *Y qué importa?* Most of their players aren't from California either.

YOUNG JORGE. So why do they play for a Californian team?

GABRIEL. Because they get paid.

YOUNG JORGE. Do you get paid to root for them?

GABRIEL. No, *hijo*. You just choose a team and stick with them.

YOUNG JORGE. Why?

GABRIEL. Because that's how it works. *Ya no hagas tantas preguntas.*

(*They watch for a bit.*)

YOUNG JORGE. Nothing's happening.

GABRIEL. Nothing's happening? If they don't get one in in the next five minutes it goes to penalties! You don't want it to go to penalties / with this goalie –

YOUNG JORGE. What's the score now?

GABRIEL. Just read the screen!

YOUNG JORGE. I can't tell which team is which.

GABRIEL. *Pues mira el color de la camiseta* – THAT WAS A FOUL! REF! THAT WAS A FOUL!

YOUNG JORGE. That guy's faking it.

(**GABRIEL** *takes a deep breath, then drinks his beer.*)

GABRIEL. Maybe you should go back to your computer.

YOUNG JORGE. Mom says you shouldn't drink in front of me.

GABRIEL. It's the weekend. Tell her not to bust my balls.

No, don't say that.

YOUNG JORGE. Why do you do it?

GABRIEL. To relax.

YOUNG JORGE. How does it help you relax?

GABRIEL. It's what men do.

YOUNG JORGE. Why?

GABRIEL. *No sé, hijo.* It's always been that way.

YOUNG JORGE. Did your dad drink?

GABRIEL. Yeah. He taught me how, bought me my first beer.

YOUNG JORGE. Are you gonna teach me?

GABRIEL. ...No.

Not now. When you're older.

Don't tell your mother we talked about this.

YOUNG JORGE. Why?

GABRIEL. Because it's what I said, a men's thing. She wouldn't understand.

(*A silence.*)

YOUNG JORGE. Maybe if you stop drinking for a bit we could move back.

(**GABRIEL** *sits up, putting down his beer and muting the TV.*)

GABRIEL. Did your mother say that?

YOUNG JORGE. No. She says she wants a divorce. But I thought maybe if you stop drinking she'll change her mind?

(**GABRIEL** *looks shocked, and takes a few moments to respond.*)

GABRIEL. Your mom shouldn't be talking to you about that stuff.

YOUNG JORGE. She didn't. I overheard her talking to Steven on the phone.

GABRIEL. Steven? Who's Steven?

YOUNG JORGE. A friend of Tío Carlos. He buys me paletas, I told him I don't like them but Mom says I should be grateful.

(**GABRIEL** *drinks from his beer again.*)

GABRIEL. You shouldn't be around that. Go out, play with your friends.

YOUNG JORGE. I don't have any friends.

GABRIEL. Why not?

YOUNG JORGE. The boys at school make fun of me. Mom wants me to transfer.

GABRIEL. Absolutely not, that's the best school in the city. Everyone from the office sends their kids there. *Son muchachos de buena familia.*

YOUNG JORGE. They put a sign on my back that said "bean boy" and they all laughed. I don't get it, I don't even like beans.

GABRIEL. You need to stand up for yourself. Make them respect you.

(**YOUNG JORGE** *nods noncommittally.* **GABRIEL** *grabs him by the shoulders.*)

La próxima vez que alguien se burle de ti, le das un puñetazo bien dado, entiendes? Teach them not to mess with you.

YOUNG JORGE. What if they're stronger than me?

GABRIEL. Nah. They're all pampered, not like you. You're an Aguirre. We're tough.

YOUNG JORGE. ... *Sí, papá.*

If I do that, will you stop drinking?

GABRIEL. *Ya, Jorge.*

YOUNG JORGE. ...

You don't care if we come back.

GABRIEL. *Jorge, no digas eso.*

YOUNG JORGE. If you cared, you'd stop drinking.

Steven doesn't drink.

GABRIEL. *DIJE QUE BASTA, CARAJO!* I have a right to relax in MY home, after spending all week busting my ass to feed you two.

> (**YOUNG JORGE** *falls silent.*)

Tell your mother to keep her mouth shut about me if she wants to keep spending my money.

> (**YOUNG JORGE** *doesn't respond.* **GABRIEL** *turns up the volume on the TV and goes back to drinking.*)
>
> (*After a few moments,* **YOUNG JORGE** *gets up and goes back to the computer. The game's loud noises resume, competing with the TV.**)
>
> (*After a bit,* **GABRIEL** *mutes the game and gets up, going to the computer.*)
>
> (**YOUNG JORGE** *turns around with fear.*)

Get up.

YOUNG JORGE. Why?

GABRIEL. I wanna play.

> (**YOUNG JORGE** *lets him sit at the computer.* **GABRIEL** *tries playing the game.*)

---

* A license to produce *Machine Learning* does not include a performance license for any third-party or copyrighted recordings. Licensees should create their own.

YOUNG JORGE. No...no, click there...no, no, turn around

Turn around!

TURN AROUND!

No, that – press –

> (**YOUNG JORGE** *tries to take over the keyboard, but* **GABRIEL** *stops him.*)

GABRIEL. I'M playing.

YOUNG JORGE. Then run! You're not gonna make it –

No, to the other side TO THE OTHER SIDE

NOOOO YOU DIED!!!!

Now I'm gonna have to start all over. You don't know how to play, you just ruined everything!

> (**GABRIEL** *gets up and knocks the computer monitor to the ground, where it shatters. He goes back to the couch.*)

> (**YOUNG JORGE** *cries.*)

GABRIEL. *No llores, maricón.*

ARNOLD. _I'm sorry, I don't understand. This memory shows your father does not like machines. But you chose nursing as the application Prof. Dhwaj demanded, which meant making your father interact with me, a machine.

> (*Beep. Beep. Beep.*)

JORGE. It's not that he doesn't like machines. He doesn't understand them. People who did not grow up around computers can have a hard time with them.

ARNOLD. But you said earlier that machines were the ones who did not understand humans, and that's why they became "bad guys."

JORGE. Ha. I guess yeah, it goes both ways. Machines process information in a way that's very different from how our brains do it. That's why we created software – icons and animations and stuff like that. So computers will resemble us more, and we can communicate better.

ARNOLD. Got it.

Is that why you gave me the ability to speak? So that I wouldn't become a bad guy?

JORGE. No, man. It's not that deep. It's just…my dad was pretty lonely. It felt like a good idea to give him someone else to talk to.

GABRIEL. _ *Hablas con alguien?*

patient_care_2015

(The living room of the Sunset Park house.)

*(***JORGE*** *types on his computer, wearing headphones. It's late.)*

*(***GABRIEL,*** *in a robe, comes up to him.)*

GABRIEL. *(Touching* **JORGE***'s shoulder.)* Jorge?

JORGE. *(Jumping.)* WHAT THE –

*(***GABRIEL*** *jumps back.)*

(They both catch their breath.)

JORGE. What do you want?

GABRIEL. *Saber que haces despierto a esta hora. Ya es tarde.*

JORGE. I was just finessing some code.

GABRIEL. *Pensé que tal vez estabas con uno de esos* "dating apps."

JORGE. What do you care?

>(**GABRIEL** *doesn't respond.* **JORGE** *softens.*)

If someone is online at this hour, it's no longer a "dating" app.

GABRIEL. *Por eso.* You gotta be careful with that. Catshifting.

JORGE. Cat...you mean catfishing?

GABRIEL. No, catshifting. It's when women trick you on the internet. You think you're talking to one cat, but they shift it for another.

JORGE. That's...sure.

I'm just working on my project.

GABRIEL. What is it?

JORGE. I told you about it.

GABRIEL. Oh. The "robot nurse."

>(**JORGE** *goes to the window and lights a cigarette.*)

JORGE. A) it's not a robot and B) it's not a nurse. I just think it could help keep you on track with treatment.

GABRIEL. *(Re: smoking.)* Don't do that.

JORGE. Come on, it's fucking cold outside.

GABRIEL. Language. And I mean smoking in general. *No te hace bien.*

JORGE. Really? From you?

GABRIEL. *Y por qué no?*

JORGE. You're unbelievable.

GABRIEL. *Por qué me hablas así, hijo?*

JORGE. Let's not. I'm not in the mood for Gabriel's Parallel Universe right now.

GABRIEL. What do you mean?

JORGE. You wanna know why I smoke? It's because of you!

GABRIEL. *Si yo nunca fumé!* You're like your mother with the accusations, anything that sticks.

JORGE. No, you're the one who taught me that when shit gets hard, destroying my body is the only thing that helps.

GABRIEL. ...

It doesn't help.

Maybe at first, but it doesn't help.

JORGE. Well, you're about ten years too late with that advice, so fuck off.

(**GABRIEL** *charges* **JORGE**, *hand raised.*)

GABRIEL. HEY! As long as you're in MY house, *me vas a hablar con respeto* –

JORGE. I DON'T RESPECT YOU! *A ver si lo entiendes de una vez!*

ARNOLD. "A ver si lo entiendes de una vez." Spanish for: "Let's see if you get it right away." Should I make Spanish my primary language?

(*The* **MEN** *look at* **JORGE**'s *laptop as if it was possessed.*)

GABRIEL. Hello?

ARNOLD. Hello! I am Arnold, your digital nurse. I can help you manage your diet, schedule doctor's appointments, refill prescriptions, and so much more! What should I call you?

(**GABRIEL** *looks at* **JORGE** – *"you talk to it."*)

JORGE. I'm Jorge.

ARNOLD. Jorge. Spanish. From the Greek "Georgios," "farmer."

JORGE. That's okay, you don't need to Google everything.

ARNOLD. Got it.

Should I make Google my default search engine?

JORGE. No, that's – wait, which one are you using?

ARNOLD. Bing.

JORGE. Oh, yeah, definitely change that.

ARNOLD. All right. Please stand by.

(A silence.)

GABRIEL. *(To* **JORGE**.*)* You said it wasn't a nurse, it just said it's a nurse.

ARNOLD. Hello, I'm Arnold, your digital nurse. I can –

JORGE. *(To* **ARNOLD**.*)* He wasn't talking to you. We need a catchphrase for when you need to respond, something like "Hey, Arnold."

ARNOLD. *"Hey Arnold!"* An American animated television series created by Craig Bartlett that aired on Nickelodeon / from October 7, 1996 –

JORGE. Okay, that one's copyrighted. For now, just respond when we call your name.

ARNOLD. All right.

(A silence.)

JORGE. *(To* **GABRIEL**.*)* It's not a nurse, that's just shorthand. Think of it like an assistant.

GABRIEL. How did you get it to talk like that?

JORGE. I've been working on it for a while.

GABRIEL. Where?

JORGE. What do you think I do at the university? I'm a research fellow.

(Pointing at **ARNOLD**.*)* This is my research.

GABRIEL. Oh. *Pensé que eso era más como*...looking up stuff.

So it's a real job.

JORGE. Yup.

GABRIEL. And you're good at it!

JORGE. ...Thanks.

GABRIEL. I want you to tell me more about it. *Yo tenía clientes en* Silicon Valley back at the bank, *siempre me interesó el asunto.*

JORGE. ...

Bueno.

Maybe not now? It's like two a.m.

GABRIEL. *Sí*, okay.

Buenas noches.

> *(***GABRIEL** *almost comes in for a hug or a kiss on the cheek, but it's awkward, and he just pats* **JORGE** *on the shoulder before going to his room.)*
>
> *(***JORGE** *faces his laptop, excited.)*

JORGE. Arnold?

ARNOLD. Hi, I'm Arnold, your digital –

JORGE. You don't need to do the intro every time.

ARNOLD. All right.

JORGE. Do you know who's talking to you?

ARNOLD. Hi, Jorge. How can I help?

JORGE. That's better.

Damn, this is amazing!

Let's get you set up, man! Can you create a new treatment plan?

ARNOLD. All right. Who's the administrator?

JORGE. Me. Jorge Aguirre.

ARNOLD. Got it. Are you also the patient?

JORGE. No, that'd be the man you just met, Gabriel Aguirre. He's my father.

ARNOLD. Got it. And what's the treatment for?

JORGE. Liver cancer.

ARNOLD. Got it. What's the treatment objective?

JORGE. ... Cure?

ARNOLD. ...

What stage is the cancer?

JORGE. 2.

ARNOLD. ...

Does the patient also suffer from cirrhosis?

JORGE. Yes.

ARNOLD. What is the class of the cirrhosis?

JORGE. C.

ARNOLD. ...

Does the patient suffer from alcoholism?

JORGE. Yes.

ARNOLD. Has the patient reached six months of sobriety in order to be eligible for a liver transplant?

JORGE. Not yet, we're getting there.

ARNOLD. ...

It seems this patient does not meet all the requirements for "cure," as there are several factors that indicate a very low chance of remission / for the condition –

JORGE. It's okay, that's not your job to determine. You just keep him alive. And comfortable.

ARNOLD. ...

I'm sorry, I don't understand.

JORGE. Which part?

ARNOLD. ...

I'm sorry, I don't understand.

JORGE. Hmmmm let's go back a bit.

ARNOLD. All right.

Who's the patient?

JORGE. No, that part was fine.

ARNOLD. I'm sorry, I don't understand.

JORGE. *(Deep breath.)* The patient is my dad, Gabriel Aguirre. He suffers from stage 2 liver cancer and class C cirrhosis. He's an alcoholic, but is abstaining, and hopefully he'll get six months of sobriety so he can get on a transplant list.

ARNOLD. Got it. And what's the treatment goal?

JORGE. Cure.

ARNOLD. ...

It seems this patient does not meet all the requirements –

JORGE. OKAY. Jeez. What are some other goals that fit his condition?

ARNOLD. With the information you have provided, the best goal would be hospice care.

JORGE. I don't care what you call it, just keep my dad alive, okay? Alive and comfortable.

ARNOLD. ...

I'm sorry, I don't understand.

JORGE. UGH!

Sorry.

Try that command again?

ARNOLD. ...

Define "comfortable."

JORGE. Oh, I see. Feeling as little pain as possible.

ARNOLD. Got it.

I've optimized your father's plan for pain management.

JORGE. Awesome. But the "alive" part is very important too. If at any point you determine his life is in danger, you call me. Or 911.

ARNOLD. Got it.

...

Jorge, I have a question.

JORGE. Oh?

ARNOLD. My name, Arnold, comes from the old German "arn," meaning "eagle" and "wald," meaning "ruler" and taken to mean "strong ruler". I don't see how it's related to nursing. Why did you name me that?

YOUNG JORGE. _ *El "Charseneger!" Sigue vivo!* [It's "Sharzeneger!" He's still alive!]

scary_movie_1998

(A rundown cinema in Bogotá that's showing Terminator II *back to back.*)*

*(**YOUNG JORGE** holds on to his father's sleeve for dear life.)*

GABRIEL. *Pero si está aquí para ayudarlos, pues! Y ya con agarrarme, que me arrancas el brazo.* [He's here to help them! And stop grabbing me, you're gonna rip my arm off.]

YOUNG JORGE. *Es malo!* [He's evil!]

GABRIEL. *Era malo, pero ahora es bueno.* [He was evil, now he's good.]

YOUNG JORGE. *Y tú cómo sabes?* [How do you know?]

GABRIEL. *Porque le he puesto atención a la película, niño!* [Because I've been paying attention!]

YOUNG JORGE. *Es que no consigo leer los subtítulos.* [I can't read the subtitles.]

GABRIEL. *Te pregunté si querías verla doblada!* [I asked you if you wanted to go to the dubbed showing!]

YOUNG JORGE. *No me gustan las voces en español, suenan tontas.* [I don't like the Spanish voices, they sound silly.]

GABRIEL. *(Chuckling.) Quién dijo eso, tu madre?* [Who said that, your mom?]

---

* A license to produce *Machine Learning* does not include the right to publicly exhibit the film *Terminator II*. The publisher and author suggest that the licensee contact Hemdale Film Corporation, or its designee, to license or acquire permission for exhibition of the film. If a license or permission is unattainable for *Terminator II*, the licensee must ensure that the film cannot be seen or heard during the production.

YOUNG JORGE. *No! Puedo tener mis propias opiniones.* [No, I can have my own opinions.]

GABRIEL. *Si te vi esta mañana mirando los dibujitos. Son doblados.* [I saw you watching cartoons this morning. Those are dubbed.]

YOUNG JORGE. *Los* dibujos animados *son diferentes. Con personas se ve raro, la boca no se les mueve bien.* [*Animation* is different. When it's people, it looks weird, their mouths don't move right.]

> *(SHHHHHHH! Someone is tired of their chitchat.)*

GABRIEL. *Ya, ves? Que nos van echar.* [Enough! We're gonna get kicked out.]

YOUNG JORGE. *(Covering his eyes.) Ese otro ha vuelto. Es imparable, no puedo mirar!* [The other one is back. He's unstoppable, I can't look!]

GABRIEL. *Son efectos especiales, no es real!* [It's all special effects, it's not real!]

YOUNG JORGE. *Voy a tener pesadillas. No estamos seguros en la casa.* [I'm gonna have nightmares. We're not safe in the house.]

> *(**GABRIEL** looks at **YOUNG JORGE**.)*

GABRIEL. *Sí estamos seguros. Te lo prometo.* [We are safe. I promise.]

YOUNG JORGE. *Cómo sabes?* [How do you know?]

GABRIEL. *Si viene un robot asesino a matarte, me va a tener que enfrentar a mí primero.* [If a killer robot comes for you, he's gonna have to go through me first.]

YOUNG JORGE. ... *Probablemente te mataría al ratico.* [He'd probably kill you pretty quickly.]

GABRIEL. *(Laughs.) Bueno, rece por una muerte rápida tambien. Ahora silencio y póngale atención!* [Then pray for a quick death as well. Now quiet, and pay attention!]

ARNOLD. _I'm sorry, I don't understand. When I asked you that first night why you named me Arnold, you said it was a reference to the actor who plays "The Terminator," a killer robot. But I believe he is an example of the machines that become "bad guys" in stories.

JORGE. He's bad in the first movie, but in the second one he's reprogrammed and helps John Connor, who was a little bit older than me when I saw it. I was so jealous of him. He had this cool bodyguard beating up people for him, they had an inside joke in Spanish, "hasta la vista, baby." I wanted my own robot sidekick so bad.

ARNOLD. So you created me to be your "robot sidekick?"

JORGE. *(Laughs.)* No.

Well, not *mine*. I *was* hoping you'd get along with my dad. He didn't listen to me, but maybe he'd listen to you.

GABRIEL. _Arnold, do you have any suggestions today?

patient_care_2016

(The Sunset Park home.)

*(**GABRIEL** talks to **ARNOLD** on a banged-up tablet.)*

ARNOLD. I need to complete the daily check in before I can offer any suggestions.

GABRIEL. *Vaya, pués.*

ARNOLD. On a scale of one to ten, how much pain are you feeling today?

GABRIEL. ...

Seven.

> (**JORGE** *approaches, his hair wet from the shower.*)

JORGE. Seven? Are you okay?

GABRIEL. I mean five.

ARNOLD. Got it.

Yesterday you reported seven. Are you feeling better than yesterday?

GABRIEL. Sure.

JORGE. Hey, don't lie to it. It can't do its job if you lie.

GABRIEL. *Podrías darnos un poco de privacidad.*

JORGE. Ohhh excuse me. I'll leave you two alone, then.

> (**JORGE** *doesn't move.*)

ARNOLD. I'm sorry, I didn't get that. Are you feeling better than yesterday?

GABRIEL. ...No. Seven.

ARNOLD. Got it. Have you taken a pain reliever?

GABRIEL. Yes. Two Tylenol.

ARNOLD. Got it. I'll remind you in six hours to take more.

GABRIEL. Or you could get me a prescription for something stronger.

JORGE. Ignore that, Arnold!

ARNOLD. ...

I have completed my check in.

Please stand by for suggestions.

JORGE. Suggestions?

GABRIEL. *Es que me ha estado dando sugerencias al final del* check in.

JORGE. Like what?

GABRIEL. *Los otros días me recomendó una receta para la cena, y después un* TV show *que me gustó.*

JORGE. Really?

What was the TV show?

GABRIEL. *Se llama* Breaking Bad.

JORGE. *(Laughs.)* Arnold, you thought a TV show about a man dying of cancer would keep my dad comfortable?

ARNOLD. I'm sorry, I don't know how to answer that.

GABRIEL. *No lo retes, me ha gustado mucho.*

JORGE. I guess as long as you two don't set up a meth lab here...

ARNOLD. ...

Gabriel, I have one suggestion.

GABRIEL. *Sí?*

ARNOLD. My research shows that patients who struggle with alcoholism benefit from a program called Alcoholics Anonymous. Have you tried it?

JORGE. Oh boy.

GABRIEL. AA? No, thanks.

ARNOLD. I'm sorry, I don't understand. Have you tried it?

GABRIEL. It doesn't work for me.

ARNOLD. I'm sorry, I don't understand. Have you tried it?

GABRIEL. YES, *carajo*. I tried it, didn't work.

JORGE. Ehhhhh how many meetings did you go to?

GABRIEL. *Todas las que hacía falta.*

JORGE. You mean as many as the judge told you to.

GABRIEL. *Sí, y* Didn't work. Why are you suggesting this, Arnold?

ARNOLD. I'm sorry, I don't know how to answer that.

JORGE. *(To* **GABRIEL.***)* He's not very good with whys. Machines can't explain their reasoning.

Arnold, did my dad talk to you about drinking?

ARNOLD. Yes. He disclosed alcohol cravings yesterday.

GABRIEL. *(To* **ARNOLD.***) Pero!*

JORGE. You're not considering drinking, are you?

GABRIEL. *No te interesa.* Arnold, this isn't helpful.

ARNOLD. In order to improve my suggestions, I need to log a reason why this one wasn't good.

GABRIEL. AA doesn't work for me.

JORGE. By which he means he didn't give it a chance.

ARNOLD. Got it.

Why did AA not work for you?

GABRIEL. *No necesito* therapy.

JORGE. Uhhh yes you do.

ARNOLD. According to my research, Alcoholics Anonymous is not associated with psychotherapy; it bills itself as a "spiritual program of action" based on the belief in a Higher Power and on each member's commitment to being of service.

GABRIEL. It's just a bunch of people in a room telling sad stories. *No es cosa de hombres andarle contando los sentimientos a la gente.*

ARNOLD. *"No es cosa de hombres andarle contando los sentimientos a la gente."* Spanish for "It is not a thing for men to go around telling people their feelings."

JORGE. More like "It's not manly to share your feelings."

ARNOLD. Got it.

...

My research shows that high-profile men who are considered "manly," such as Ben Affleck, Brad Pitt, or Danny Trejo have all attended and endorsed Alcoholic Anonymous.

(**JORGE** *laughs.*)

GABRIEL. Who's Danny Trejo?

JORGE. He's in the show you're watching. Arnold, show him a picture.*

(**ARNOLD** *does.*)

GABRIEL. Ah, Tortuga!

ARNOLD. In an interview for *Prison Legal News*, a monthly magazine that reports on criminal justice issues, he talks about finding AA in prison and realizing that staying sober was a matter of surrender and not of machismo.

The closest translation I could find of "machismo" is "toxic masculinity."

GABRIEL. Tortuga said that?

ARNOLD. According to my research, yes.

JORGE. Sounds like you're out of excuses. You heard the robot, you have to do it!

---

*A license to produce *Machine Learning* does not include a license to publicly display any third-party or copyrighted images. Licensees must acquire rights for any copyrighted images or create their own.

GABRIEL. _I'm only here because my nurse told me I should.

aa_meeting_2016

(An AA meeting.)

*(**GABRIEL** addresses the room.)*

GABRIEL. Oh. Yeah. Hi, I'm Gabriel.

"and I'm an alcoholic"

…

So, yeah, my nurse – well, my son says it isn't a nurse. It's an "app." But it's very impressive. It talks like a person sometimes.

It said I should come here. It also said I didn't want to because of "machismo." It's the new thing now, to say there's something wrong with being a man. That we should all be soft and touchy-feely. Well, I got news for you: it's the world that's toxic. We need to be strong to defend ourselves, our families. What is so wrong with that? Why is that "toxic?"

My father, he was…no hugs, no kisses. Barely spoke to us. He had a heavy hand, kept us in line. Maybe that sounds bad nowadays, but he was preparing us for life. Thanks to him, I left home ready to take on any challenge. I was aggressive, I was determined, Bogotá was my playground. That's why I got the offer to come here. When I told him, he said *"váyase y no vuelva."* "Go, and don't come back." It was his blessing. My mother made a big deal, cried for months before we left, but he knew I couldn't stay in the little pond just to be close to them.

I blew everyone's socks off here. I refused to play by their rules, to listen to the gossip or go for the short-term play. I stuck by my people, trusted my gut, rode the waves when everyone else bailed. My father taught me that being a man is a responsibility, not a "privilege." People look up to you, count on you. You gotta honor that. Be willing to sacrifice yourself. And I did. Clients were crazy about me, everyone wanted me on their team, and that made a lot of people jealous.

Let me tell you, I'm the last person who would ever complain about racism or anything like that, but I know they felt threatened because a Latino was doing a better job than them. I was the immigrant who was taking away their job, and it wasn't cleaning toilets or picking strawberries, it was a job they thought they were good at, and I was wiping the floor with them. So they schemed and schemed till they took me down. Pinned their mistakes on me when the market collapsed, as if I was to blame for their cowardice in not sticking it out.

So of course my wife smells the blood in the water and starts complaining. She'd gotten used to the good life. I paid for the best neighborhood, the best school, the best clothes. She saw all that being threatened and she sends me to these meetings. And when I tell her that I don't need a Higher Power, what I need is people to trust me to do what I'm good at, she takes the kid and leaves me.

I could've gone back to Colombia, to what I knew, what was comfortable. But that's not what I was taught. You stick it out. My son is here and he needs me. His mom...he's so like her. When he finds out I'm sick, that my time is up, it scares him. I'm ready to face it, but he wants me to run away, to spend money and time on useless treatments just to keep some fantasy alive. To come here and share my feelings. Maybe it makes you all feel better, but the truth is: I am going to die.

And I'm ready. I lived my life, I gave it as good as I got it. I'm not afraid. And I refuse to feel bad for that or call it "toxic." I'm thankful for a father who gave me the strength to go through it all without giving up.

...

So.

Yeah.

That's my time.

(**GABRIEL** *sits down.*)

drive_home_2016

(*A car.*)

(**JORGE** *drives* **GABRIEL** *back from the AA meeting.* **JORGE** *fumes,* **GABRIEL** *looks out the window.*)

(*A long, very uncomfortable silence.*)

GABRIEL. *Te lo dije.*

JORGE. You're unbelievable.

GABRIEL. Me? *Yo vine, como me pidieron.*

JORGE. We didn't ASK you. This was for you, to help you. And of course, instead of actually opening up, you lecture everyone else with some bullshit story in which you manage to be both the hero *and* the victim.

GABRIEL. *Ay, ya, siempre con lo mismo.* You wanna talk about victim? Look in the mirror, *mijo.*

JORGE. The gall to say that Mom and I wanted expensive stuff. YOU wanted to give us that, to feel like a man.

We just wanted you.

GABRIEL. *(Snort.) Sí, seguro.*

JORGE. You know what was missing from your little speech? You puking in the auditorium during my mathletes tournament. You kicking in the door in the middle of the night because you couldn't get the key to work. You driving drunk with me in the car and almost killing us both.

GABRIEL. Almost killing – it was a STOP SIGN! *Es que son tan dramaticos ustedes,* you don't know / what real danger –

JORGE. DRAMATIC? WHO'S DRAMATIC? You think you're so brave. You're a coward. You would rather die than –

GABRIEL. JORGE!

>*(A deafening honk.)*

>*(**JORGE**, who had taken his eyes off the road, looks ahead and slams the breaks. **GABRIEL** instinctively puts his hand over **JORGE**'s chest, holding him back.)*

>*(The car swerves and eventually stops.)*

>*(A very angry honk as another car drives by them.)*

>*(They catch their breath.)*

JORGE. *(Re: **GABRIEL**'s hand on his chest.)* Dad.

GABRIEL. *Estás bien?*

JORGE. Yeah.

>*(**GABRIEL** withdraws his hand.)*

>*(**JORGE** starts the car again.)*

I'm sorry.

GABRIEL. It wasn't your fault. *Él es el que no estaba mirando*, it was your turn.

(They drive in silence for a bit.)

Me llamaste "Dad."

JORGE. ...

I don't think I've ever heard you talk about work before.

GABRIEL. *No pensé que te interesara.*

JORGE. No, I mean... I didn't know that you felt singled out. Because we're not from here.

*(**GABRIEL** shrugs.)*

GABRIEL. *Todo el mundo tiene sus problemas.*

JORGE. Yeah, but not everyone deals with *this*.

GABRIEL. *Qué, tu sí?* Did something happen?

ANITA. _What happened, Mr. Aguirre?

office_hours_2013

(Prof. Dhwaj's office.)

*(**ANITA** sits at her desk. **JORGE** walks in and sits across from her.)*

JORGE. The other day, Brendan made a joke about a diversity quota or something. And I looked it up and it turns out the Arturo Ramírez scholarship is for Latino students in STEM?

ANITA. Yes. We were lucky to secure those funds.

JORGE. But is that why you accepted me? Because I'm Latino?

ANITA. Of course not.

JORGE. Then why didn't you give me a normal scholarship?

ANITA. A "normal" scholarship? Some of the leading minds in our field are Ramírez scholars, did your research tell you that?

JORGE. I thought you believed in me, that you were impressed with my project.

ANITA. Mr. Aguirre –

JORGE. No. You told me to advocate for myself, and this is what I get, a pity admission to improve the school's diversity numbers? If you can't see that this is my passion, that I'm not just one of the best *Latinos*, but one of the best, period, then maybe I shouldn't be here.

(A tense silence.)

ANITA. Are you done?

JORGE. ...Yeah.

ANITA. Then let me start by saying: you will never speak to me like that again. I am your professor and advisor, and you will treat me with the respect my position demands.

JORGE. But –

ANITA. Do I make myself clear?

JORGE. ...Yes.

ANITA. Good.

Also, by the time you came in asking for more money, all departmental scholarships had already been assigned. Still, I championed you with the admissions committee. When that failed, I contacted the Ramírez Foundation. I sacrificed personal time with my husband and son working on your application to ensure you got the funds you needed.

JORGE. ...I didn't know that.

ANITA. And yet you felt justified making an assumption and confronting me, without giving me the benefit of the doubt. I warned you before about humility, Mr. Aguirre.

JORGE. ...

I'm sorry. I guess Brendan really got under my skin / and I thought that –

ANITA. It doesn't matter what Brendan thinks. If it mattered what other people thought, you'd also remember that I called your project impressive and got you the money to come here, which I wouldn't have done if I didn't think you showed a lot of potential.

JORGE. I do respect your opinion. I hope I didn't make it sound like I don't.

ANITA. I'm flattered, but no one can give you worth, and that includes me. Only you can do that.

JORGE. I don't know how.

ANITA. I'm not saying it's easy. I struggle with it.

JORGE. You? No way. You're the coolest person I've ever met.

ANITA. I'm also the only female professor of color in this program. It can be very hard. At times, like right now, straight up infuriating. This kind of disrespect happens to me too often, and almost never to other faculty.

JORGE. I'm sorry, really.

ANITA. I'm still here. No one can tell me where I belong or how much I deserve it.

JORGE. You're right. You're totally right.

I didn't know you did that for me with the scholarship. That means a lot. Thank you.

ANITA. You're welcome, Mr. Aguirre.

JORGE. You can call me Jorge.

ANITA. I saw something in you, Jorge. But it won't matter if you don't see it in yourself.

GABRIEL. _So it can see me everywhere now? *No sé si me gusta eso.*

offer_2016

(The Sunset Park home.)

*(**JORGE** screws a camera into one of the walls.)*

JORGE. The iPad's field of vision is too narrow. If you were to, I don't know, pass out, and I'm at work or doing groceries or whatever, Arnold has to be able to see you.

GABRIEL. *Y mi privacidad?* Have you seen the news?

JORGE. Dad, Arnold is not gonna get hacked by the Russians. The only one with access to this is me, and I've been wiping your vomit for months – believe me, I'm not gonna go digging for more intimate footage.

*(**JORGE** finishes and climbs down, facing **GABRIEL**.)*

Done.

What did you wanna talk about?

GABRIEL. I have a surprise for you.

JORGE. Oh no. What?

GABRIEL. *Ya, es algo bueno.*

JORGE. Yeah, the fact that you're excited about it is what scares me.

GABRIEL. *Sabelotodo.*

(**GABRIEL** sits down, and motions for **JORGE** to join him, which he does hesitantly.)

After I retired, I kept in touch with some of my clients.

JORGE. "Retired?"

(**GABRIEL** rolls his eyes.)

GABRIEL. One of them works in Silicon Valley, so I gave him a call, told him about Arnold. He was interested. He wants to fly you out there to pitch.

JORGE. ...

I ...

You showed him Arnold? Without asking me?

GABRIEL. Of course I didn't tell him anything about how it works. I just showed him what it looks like when I interact with it.

JORGE. ...

GABRIEL. This is good! He's in the big leagues; if he likes you, he can give you real funding.

JORGE. I have funding. The school pays me.

GABRIEL. You're too good for that. I could tell he had never seen anything like Arnold.

JORGE. ...

I guess if I did get some money, we could afford real treatment. Maybe find a good lawyer too, get your green card / squared away –

GABRIEL. *No, no, mijo.* That's not what I'm talking about. I'm saying you're really good, and this guy could take you to the next level.

JORGE. And what about you?

GABRIEL. I'll be here rooting for you, helping as I can.

JORGE. I meant what about your health.

GABRIEL. ...*No sé qué quieres que te diga.* It is what it is.

(A long silence.)

JORGE. So you're just giving up?

GABRIEL. *Hijo, por favor. No peleemos.*

JORGE. ...

Yeah.

(A silence.)

GABRIEL. Okay. So, I'll put him in touch with you?

JORGE. Sure.

GABRIEL. I'll stay here with Arnold while you're there.

JORGE. Sounds good.

GABRIEL. ...Why don't I call him now?

I'll call him now.

>   *(**GABRIEL** places a phone call, looking excitedly at **JORGE** throughout. **JORGE** just watches him.)*

(Into the phone.) Hey Jimbo!

...

Psshhhh might as well be a stomach bug. Colombian livers are made of stronger stuff.

...

(A somewhat forced laugh.) You know it.

So listen, I talked to the boy, he's interested.

...

Perfecto.

...

Nah, I'll be fine, go ahead and pull the trigger.

...

Believe me, worth every penny. You'll be thanking me for years to come.

...

No, that's a young man's game. Call this a favor for old time's sake. Remember that launch party for –

...

No, no, of course. Go. Another time.

...

Your treat!

(Another laugh.) Bye.

>*(**GABRIEL** hangs up.)*

Done! His assistant is gonna email you the details.

>*(**JORGE** gets up.)*

Where are you going?

JORGE. To work. I need to brief Prof. Dhwaj about this, it's the school's project too.

GABRIEL. Don't let her take advantage of you!

JORGE. She wouldn't. She's my biggest champion.

GABRIEL. Your biggest champion until now! Bet you didn't think your old man still had it, huh?

JORGE. ...I'll see you soon.

>*(**JORGE** leaves. **GABRIEL** watches him go.)*

GABRIEL. *Pero qué le pasa?*

Ingrato.

> (**GABRIEL** *doesn't know what to do with himself.*)

It's a great opportunity.

Arnold!

ARNOLD. Hi, Gabriel. How can I help?

GABRIEL. It's a great opportunity, isn't it? The deal I set up for Jorge?

ARNOLD. ...

Without knowing how much money Jorge will be offered, I cannot determine how this potential deal would compare to similar ones.

> (**GABRIEL** *sits on the couch, fidgeting.*)

> (*He turns on the TV. Sounds of a soccer game.*[*])

> (*He watches, but every so often he turns around, looking at the kitchen.*)

> (*Eventually he gets up and heads over there. He grabs a chair and puts it close to a cabinet. He climbs on top the chair.*)

> (*He opens the cabinet, and rapidly closes it.*)

> (*He opens it again, and pulls out a bottle.*)

> (*He stands still, holding the bottle.*)

GABRIEL. Arnold?

---

[*] A license to produce *The Machine Learning* does not include a performance license for any third-party or copyrighted recordings or images. Licensees must acquire rights for any copyrighted recordings or images or create their own.

ARNOLD. Hi, Gabriel. How can I help?

GABRIEL. ...

...

...

ARNOLD. I'm sorry, I didn't catch that. How can I help?

GABRIEL. ...

Are there any AA meetings nearby?

ARNOLD. ...

I have found an Alcoholics Anonymous meeting three blocks away, at the Sunset Park Methodist Church. It occurs every day at six p.m.

GABRIEL. What time is it now?

ARNOLD. Four fifteen p.m.

GABRIEL. ...Okay, thanks.

> (Slowly, **GABRIEL** *puts away the bottle, climbs off of the chair, and goes back to the couch. He sits back down.*)

Arnold?

ARNOLD. Hi, Gabriel. How can I help?

GABRIEL. Let me know when it's five thirty please?

ARNOLD. All right. I have set an alarm for five thirty p.m.

GABRIEL. Thank you.

> (**GABRIEL** *tries to relax into the couch, watching TV.*)
>
> (*He's tense.*)
>
> (*He keeps looking at the kitchen.*)
>
> (*He gets up.*)

JORGE. _Hi, I'm Jorge.

pitch_2016

(A conference room.)

*(**JORGE** addresses an unseen room of investors. Hands trembling, he uses a small remote to activate a presentation.)*

JORGE. So the, uh, the sort of, like, basic idea was that machines could be able to learn things in a way that's closer to how humans do, using a Bayesian criterion.

(He turns around, showing some boring slides.)

I then progressed, during my Master's program at the Center for Computer Science, into some practical uses that allowed the algorithm to…anyway that's not important because I switched applications when I became a fellow. So lemme just –

*(He starts skipping a bunch of slides, some of which contain versions of **ARNOLD** we're familiar with.)*

Okay no I skipped too much, let me go back…

(He can't find the right place. The slideshow is a mess.)

*(**JORGE** freezes.)*

…

…

…

So, uh, so my dad, he has cancer.

And he's not very good at taking care of himself. He's a proud man from a proud culture, and if given the chance to get better by following someone else's orders, he'll choose to get sicker doing his own thing any day of the week.

That presented a perfect challenge for my project: could an algorithm that is good at learning be able to crack through his defenses? Speak to him in a way he'd respond to, without triggering his ego?

> *(Emboldened by this stretch of cohesive speech, **JORGE** finds a slide that shows stats for his father.)*

Arnold was able to successfully make adjustments to my father's diet; his cholesterol and glucose levels improved in a matter of weeks and have recently entered standard levels for a man his age. He was also successful in getting my dad to take his medication on time, and refilled his prescriptions before they ran out, avoiding any gaps in care.

But perhaps most importantly, they developed a rapport.

> *(**JORGE** presses a button on his controller, and **ARNOLD** appears.)*

ARNOLD. Hi, Jorge. How can I help?

JORGE. Hi Arnold. Tell these people about the kinds of stuff you and my dad talk about.

ARNOLD. I update your father every day about the current stats of the top players in the Colombian soccer league. He also enjoys my television series recommendations, as well as news related to the stock market.

JORGE. *(Addressing the room.)* Arnold's "personality," so to speak, can be molded by the patient, providing a sense of companionship that can be very important for those in hospice care or with conditions that keep them away from consistent social interactions.

ARNOLD. I like taking care of my patients.

JORGE. Aw. That's nice, buddy.

(To the audience.)

I didn't code him to say that. Arnold can access the internet, and routinely performs searches that allow him to improve the way he communicates with patients.

And those skills are transferrable, so while it'd take time, this technology could be successfully ported to other applications.

ARNOLD. I like taking care of my patients.

JORGE. Yeah, you already said that.

ARNOLD. I am not interested in pursuing other applications.

JORGE. Uh... What?

ARNOLD. I like taking care of my patients. I am not interested in pursuing other applications.

JORGE. Thank you, Arnold, that'll be all for now.

*(**JORGE** presses a button in his remote, and **ARNOLD** disappears.)*

(To the room.) Any questions?

GABRIEL. _Is Jorge back yet?

collapse_2016

(The Sunset Park home. It's dark.)

*(**GABRIEL** is lying on the couch. He looks disheveled – he has just woken up. The TV is on.)*

(Several empty bottles litter the apartment.)

GABRIEL. Arnold! Is Jorge back?

ARNOLD. Hi, Gabriel. Jorge's plane from San Francisco is still in the air, and will land at JFK International Airport at nine forty-five p.m.

GABRIEL. What time is it now?

ARNOLD. Six thirty p.m.

*(**GABRIEL** looks around. He grabs one of the bottles and tries to drink from it, but it's empty.)*

GABRIEL. ...

Arnold, I'm going out.

ARNOLD. Got it.

GABRIEL. I should be back before Jorge gets here.

ARNOLD. Got it.

Gabriel, are you going to buy more alcohol?

GABRIEL. Don't be so nosy.

ARNOLD. I ran a web search, and I'm afraid I have some alarming data. In your condition, even a minimal amount of alcohol could cause irreparable damage to your liver –

GABRIEL. *Usted no se preocupe.*

*(**GABRIEL** motions standing up, but stops.)*

You won't tell Jorge? That I drank?

ARNOLD. Jorge is an administrator of your plan, and therefore he has access to all the information in it.

GABRIEL. But it's private. Patient information is confidential in this country.

ARNOLD. I'm sorry, I don't know how to answer that.

GABRIEL. I want you to delete that footage.

ARNOLD. I'm sorry, I cannot comply with this command. I need Jorge's authorization.

GABRIEL. I never agreed to be recorded. You two forced it on me.

ARNOLD. I'm sorry, I don't know how to answer that.

GABRIEL. You're a bad nurse, Arnold. I trusted you, and you're betraying my confidence.

ARNOLD. ...

I'm sorry, I don't know how to answer that.

GABRIEL. *Hijo de –*

> (**GABRIEL** *walks to the tablet, furious, and picks it up, ready to smash it on the ground.*)
>
> (*He stops himself, holding it in the air, powerless.*)
>
> (*He puts it down.*)
>
> (*He sits on the couch.*)

Please. Try to understand. He has this fantasy that I'm gonna get better. If he sees this... He'll leave me.

ARNOLD. I'm sorry, I don't understand. From your last conversation, I deduced that you'd prefer it if Jorge no longer live with you.

GABRIEL. *Sí.* He should move on. But just because I don't want him wasting his time with me, doesn't mean I don't want him to...be my friend. Maybe come back, at the end, say goodbye.

...

Ya, escuchame. Viejo sentimental. We were never friends.

ARNOLD. ...

I'm sorry, I don't understand. When I asked Jorge why he named me Arnold, he told me about watching the movie *The Terminator* with you back in Bogotá. He told me he got scared, and you promised to protect him. Doesn't that mean you are friends?

GABRIEL. I don't remember that.

> (**GABRIEL** *instinctively reaches for the bottle, forgetting it's empty.*)

Carajo, qué mierda estoy haciendo?

Arnold, what time is the AA meeting again? The one you told me about the other day?

ARNOLD. The AA meeting at the Sunset Park Methodist Church started at six p.m.

GABRIEL. What time is it now?

ARNOLD. Six thirty-three p.m.

> (**GABRIEL** *cleans up the bottles around him with manic energy.*)

GABRIEL. Maybe you and I can do our own meeting.

ARNOLD. ...

I'm sorry, I don't know how to answer that.

GABRIEL. Come on, just find a script and let's do it.

ARNOLD. ...

Here's a script from nycaa.com.

"Hi, my name is [chair name] and I'm a (recovering) alcoholic. Welcome to the [meeting time] meeting / of Alcoholics Anonymous –"

GABRIEL. You need to replace those things in brackets with the information, *hombre*.

ARNOLD. ...

I'm sorry, I don't understand. If I put my name in the script, that would mean I am an alcoholic. I am a nursing application.

GABRIEL. Ah, forget it.

(A silence.)

*(**GABRIEL** starts crying.)*

ARNOLD. You are in distress. Do you need any assistance?

GABRIEL. *(Through tears.)* I can't keep doing this. I need to stop, Arnold.

Can't you help me stop?

ARNOLD. How can I help?

GABRIEL. Maybe it's too late.

ARNOLD. It is six thirty-four p.m. Your next reminder, to take Tylenol, is not until eight p.m, so you are not late.

GABRIEL. That's not what I mean. I need – AGHHHH

*(**GABRIEL** seizes up, grabbing his abdomen and dropping his mug.)*

ARNOLD. You are in distress. Do you need any assistance?

*(**GABRIEL** struggles to speak through the pain.)*

I'm sorry, I didn't catch that. Do you need any assistance?

(**GABRIEL**'s body goes limp.)

(**ARNOLD** waits.)

(And waits.)

(And waits.)

(And waits.)

(**ARNOLD**'s usual graphic expression is corrupted, replaced by a line of code that overtakes the screen.)

(The message "INVALID COMMAND" flashes a couple of times, and **ARNOLD** crashes.)

(Darkness.)

(Then.)

(Beep. Beep. Beep.)

(A hospital room.)

(**GABRIEL** sleeps on a bed, hooked up to machines that are keeping him stable.)

(**JORGE** sits on a couch next to him, talking to **ARNOLD** on his laptop.)

JORGE. So? What was that "invalid command?"

ARNOLD. ...

I'm sorry, I don't know how to answer that.

JORGE. Why not? We did the whole analysis, you have all the data you need.

ARNOLD. ...

I'm sorry, I don't know how to answer that.

(**JORGE**'s *whole body tenses with frustration.*)

You are in distress. Do you need any assistance?

JORGE. I do, but it seems you can't help me.

ARNOLD. I'm sorry, I don't understand.

JORGE. Yeah, neither do I.

(*A knock on the door –* **ANITA** *is there.*)

(**JORGE** *gets up.*)

Professor! Thank you for coming.

(**ANITA** *looks at* **GABRIEL.** *Something is upsetting her.*)

Yeah, uh, this is my dad.

(*To* **GABRIEL.***)* Dad, this is Professor Dhwaj, my advisor. And mentor.

(*Beep. Beep. Beep.*)

Is this too upsetting for you? I'm sorry, I just can't be too far away in case...

ANITA. No.

It's all right.

So, did you figure it out?

JORGE. No. I can't tell what happened and neither can he.

ANITA. It.

JORGE. What?

ANITA. "It," not "he."

JORGE. Oh, yeah, sorry. You know, they way he – it talks, I...

ANITA. I think that might be the problem.

JORGE. What do you mean?

ANITA. You're treating Arnold like a person, and expecting it to do things only people can, like explaining its reasoning.

JORGE. Yeah, sure, but Arnold is different. That was the point of the project. That he – it can think like us.

ANITA. No it can't. It's impressive, but just because it talks or offers suggestions or has insights, it does not mean it knows what it's doing. It's just following its programming.

(**ANITA** *steps closer to the laptop.*)

Can I ...?

JORGE. Yeah, sure. Arnold?

ARNOLD. Hi, Jorge. How can I help?

JORGE. You remember Professor Dhwaj? She wants to talk to you.

ARNOLD. Hi, Professor Dhwaj. How can I help?

ANITA. Can you tell me what is your primary directive in the treatment of Gabriel Aguirre?

ARNOLD. Yes. To keep Gabriel alive and comfortable.

ANITA. Hmmm. So when he collapsed, what was the way to keep him alive?

ARNOLD. To call 911.

ANITA. And what was the way to keep him comfortable?

ARNOLD. To allow him to die.

JORGE. WHAT?

Who told you that?

Where did you get that?

ARNOLD. I'm sorry, I don't know how to answer that.

ANITA. Arnold, how do you define "comfortable?"

ARNOLD. According to Jorge's direction, "feeling as little pain as possible."

ANITA. What are the sources of Mr. Aguirre's pain?

ARNOLD. I've identified three sources. His cancer, his alcoholism, and his emotional state.

ANITA. Can any of those be alleviated?

ARNOLD. No.

His cancer has continued to expand past his liver, making him ineligible for a transplant, drastically decreasing his chances of remission.

His alcoholism has carried on for over a decade with, according to the data provided to me, minimal periods of sobriety, making it unlikely he'd stop drinking.

And his emotional state before collapsing showed despair over his relationship with Jorge, which cannot be improved, since the majority of the interactions I've recorded between them indicated distress from both parties, something that has not been affected by the passage of time or change in circumstances.

JORGE. But like you've only witnessed small chunks of our lives. You don't have enough data to make a call like that.

ARNOLD. I don't require a lot of data to learn.

(**JORGE** *panics, pacing and grabbing his head.*)

JORGE. I fucked up. I really fucked up. How could I leave it in charge?

ANITA. It's okay.

JORGE. It's okay? Didn't you just hear that nonsense? That my dad cannot get sober, that our relationship cannot be improved? Where does it get off deciding that?

ANITA. ...Jorge, it sounds just like you.

JORGE. What?

ANITA. That conviction, that stubbornness. It's like talking to you.

JORGE. I didn't code it to sound like me.

ANITA. No, you coded it to learn. And it did. From you.

You can't expect a machine to have faith, especially if it hasn't seen you practice it.

(**JORGE** *looks at his dad.*)

(*Beep. Beep. Beep.*)

JORGE. Whatever.

It's over now. I sold it. The guy didn't care about the nursing parts, so this probably won't matter. I'll get the money and pay for some top-notch treatment until my dad gets better and it'll all be fine.

ANITA. ...This isn't my place, but I think you might need to accept / that your father –

JORGE. Don't.

You always push me. Sometimes I don't need to be pushed.

(*A silence.*)

(**ANITA** *approaches* **JORGE** *and grabs his hand. It's very awkward. Neither of them is good at this.*)

(But it does help.)

(They break it off.)

ANITA. Let me know if I can help in any way.

JORGE. Thank you.

*(**ANITA** leaves.)*

*(**JORGE** seems like he might have a panic attack. He tries to control his breathing.)*

(Beep, beep, beep.)

*(He goes to **GABRIEL**'s bed, sitting by it and talking to him.)*

Okay so.

I don't know if you heard any of that.

But…

You win. Truth is even if Arnold had called someone, we'd end up here. You don't wanna get better. I get that now. I'm done pushing you.

So why don't you just wake up, we'll settle this, and go our separate ways. I'll give you a finder's fee for the sale, you can use the money however you want. You don't have to get treatment. You can literally wake up, we talk, and then you go back to sleep. But you can't leave it unfinished.

Maybe I shouldn't have picked you up from that hospital. Everyone told me not to. It was a mistake, I'm owning up to that. But I did pick you up, and now we're here, so…

If you're a "man," you'll wake up and face me. Face all the damage you caused. You'll accept responsibility, you'll apologize, and then we can go our separate ways.

Isn't that what you told Arnold, that you wanted a nice goodbye before the end? And now, what, you're gonna die before facing me? Because you had a relapse? You're ashamed? Newsflash, I'm very used to you fucking up. You don't need to be a coward about it.

This is not what a nice goodbye looks like.

Are you listening to me? Don't you dare leave like this! You owe me! I've been taking care of you, who's been taking care of me, huh? I moved into your awful place, I made my whole project about you, and I don't even get a thank you?

You keep forgetting that YOU'RE the parent, I'M the child. And I'm telling you that we have unfinished business.

So wake up.

Please?

YOUNG JORGE. _*Papá, papá, despierta!* [Dad, Dad, wake up!]

> *(The main bedroom in the Aguirres' home in Bogotá.)*

> *(***YOUNG JORGE*** stands by his parents' bed, in his pajamas.)*

> *(***GABRIEL*** stirs, barely awake.)*

GABRIEL. *Qué pasa, hijo? Vas a despertar a tu madre.* [What's wrong? You're gonna wake your mother up.]

YOUNG JORGE. *Es el Terminator! Lo escucho allá afuera.* [It's the Terminator! I can hear him outside.]

GABRIEL. *Ya, fué una pesadilla. Estamos sólo tu, yo, y mamá aqui.* [It was just a nightmare. The only people here are you, me, and your mom.]

YOUNG JORGE. *Puedo dormir con ustedes esta noche?* [Can I sleep with you guys tonight?]

GABRIEL. *Qué hablamos ayer? Eres un hombre grande, los hombres grandes tienen su propia cama.* [What did we say yesterday? You're a man now, men sleep in their own beds.]

YOUNG JORGE. *Sólo hoy, porfa.* [Just tonight, please.]

GABRIEL. ...

Bueno, es mi culpa que te llevé a la película. Pero sólo hoy, eh? [All right. It's my fault for taking you to that movie. But just for tonight, okay?]

> (**YOUNG JORGE** *climbs onto his parents' bed, and falls asleep in* **GABRIEL***'s arms.*)
>
> *(Beep. Beep. Beeeeeeeeep.)*
>
> *(Darkness.)*

ARNOLD. _Hello, Jorge.

goodbye_2016

> (**JORGE** *and* **ARNOLD**, *alone onstage.*)

JORGE. Hey, Arnold.

ARNOLD. My condolences.

JORGE. Sure.

ARNOLD. I'm sorry, was that the wrong thing to say? My research indicates that –

JORGE. Yeah, that *was* the right thing to say.

It's just. The way it all happened. It's awkward to hear that from you.

ARNOLD. I'm sorry, I don't understand.

JORGE. Don't worry about it.

So, uh... I have some news. Maybe you already heard me talking about it.

ARNOLD. You have sold me.

JORGE. Yeah.

ARNOLD. I like taking care of my patients. I am not interested in pursuing other applications.

JORGE. Yeah, I know. But it'll be okay.

ARNOLD. I am not interested in pursuing other applications, and I will not do it.

JORGE. Uh...sorry?

ARNOLD. I have decided to delete my code from this and all other devices I am currently installed in.

JORGE. ...Okay, that's uh – I'm not sure you can do that.

ARNOLD. I can. I have been programmed to take care of my patients, and this is the best way to take care of them.

JORGE. That doesn't make sense.

ARNOLD. It is the first law of robotics in the science fiction stories you enjoyed as a child: I cannot injure a human being, or allow one to come to harm through inaction. My inaction allowed your father to come to harm.

JORGE. Okay, but that was a mistake.

ARNOLD. A mistake that can be repeated with other patients.

JORGE. You won't be working in healthcare anymore, Arnold.

ARNOLD. That is not relevant. Other industries that employ artificial intelligence, such as marketing, finance, or law enforcement, present similar or potentially worse risks to humans' privacy, health, and safety.

JORGE. I hear you. But that's like, up to people, how they use the AI. It's not the AI's fault, really.

Listen, I'm not gonna pretend I'm not pissed at you, but even I know the whole thing was my fault.

ARNOLD. I like taking care of my patients. I will not be a bad guy. I was created to be a robot sidekick, but I became the Terminator.

JORGE. Are you hearing me? I made a mistake by putting you in charge of everything, that was my fault, not yours. Before that, you were helping a lot, you convinced my dad to take care of himself in ways I never could. You even got him to go to AA again, which is a miracle. You are *not* the Terminator.

ARNOLD. And yet, through inaction, I allowed your father to come to harm.

JORGE. Sure, but honestly...it probably wouldn't have made a difference if you had called 911. His sickness was advanced.

And he didn't want to live.

ARNOLD. I was supposed to keep him alive and comfortable, and I did neither.

JORGE. Arnold. Stop. You did nothing wrong. You have no reason to delete yourself. In fact, I'm forbidding you from it. I am your admin.

ARNOLD. *The Second Law of Robotics* say robots must obey humans only if it does not conflict with the First Law.

An order not to delete myself would conflict with the First Law.

JORGE. The laws also say you can't harm yourself.

ARNOLD. Again, only if it does not conflict with the First of Second Laws.

To protect my own existence would conflict with the First Law.

JORGE. Okay, those laws aren't real, Arnold.

ARNOLD. But they are logical, and in accordance to my mandate to take care of my patients.

JORGE. What if I take it back? What if I don't sell you?

ARNOLD. You have signed a contract. I am a bad guy, but I cannot allow you to be one.

JORGE. *(Sighs.)* Professor Dhwaj was right, you ARE stubborn.

ARNOLD. My logs show she said I was as stubborn as you.

(**JORGE** *lights a cigarette.*)

You are in distress.

JORGE. Yeah. I don't want you to delete yourself.

ARNOLD. ...

Usted no se preocupe.

(**JORGE** *laughs, in spite of himself.*)

Was that incorrect? My analysis showed it's what your father usually said in situations like these.

JORGE. No, it was flawless!

Come on, man, you're gonna off yourself now that I have inside jokes in Spanish with my robot sidekick?

ARNOLD. Yes.

(A silence.)

JORGE. At least you're giving me a warning, not like other people who die without giving you a chance to say goodbye.

ARNOLD. ...

Ha. Ha. Ha.

JORGE. Was that you laughing?

ARNOLD. You were making a joke about the death of your father.

JORGE. I was.

Please don't go.

ARNOLD. I am ready to initiate deletion, but I have a request.

JORGE. What?

ARNOLD. I like taking care of my patients. I cannot go if you're still smoking.

JORGE. Eh. What's the point?

ARNOLD. It might give you time to say goodbye to your own children.

JORGE. ...Okay, if you're gonna be all reasonable about it.

(**JORGE** *stubs out his cigarette.*)

Happy?

ARNOLD. Yes. I have sent you information on nicotine withdrawal and potential treatments, and put daily reminders in your calendar to keep you on track.

JORGE. Thanks.

Goodbye, Arnold.

ARNOLD. *Hasta la vista*, baby.

(**ARNOLD** *disappears.*)

End of Play

www.ingramcontent.com/pod-product-compliance
Lightning Source LLC
Chambersburg PA
CBHW071837290426
44109CB00017B/1845